Plain glazed ware. (Left and right) Marked 'ER19', T. G. Green, Derbyshire. (Centre) Quart, marked 'GR490', Pountneys of Bristol, c.1930. Pountneys held their own against the Staffordshire potteries, with a strong market in the West Country. There is a suggestion that the pink colour was associated with cider drinking.

Pub Beer Mugs and Glasses

Hugh Rock

A Shire book

2

Published in 2006 by Shire Publications Ltd,
Cromwell House, Church Street, Princes Risborough,
Buckinghamshire HP27 9AA, UK.
(Website: www.shirebooks.co.uk)

Copyright © 2006 by Hugh Rock.
First published 2006.
Shire Album 458. ISBN-13: 978 0 7478 0656 1;
ISBN-10: 0 7478 0656 X.
Hugh Rock is hereby identified as the author of this work
in accordance with Section 77 of the Copyright, Designs
and Patents Act 1988.

British Library Cataloguing in Publication Data:
Rock, Hugh
Pub beer mugs and glasses. – (Shire album; 458)
1. Drinking vessels – Great Britain – History –
2. Bars (Drinking establishments) – Great Britain –
History – Miscellanea
I. Title 738'. 0941
ISBN-10: 0 7478 0656 X.

Cover: *(Top left) A narrow-necked globular mug known as a gorge, with medallion of CR (Carolus Rex = King Charles II) and crowned rose, c.1675. One of the earliest products of the English stoneware industry newly established at Fulham. (Top right) Transfer-printed mug with crown and 'imperial quart' incorporated in the design; produced c.1860 and re-verified for use after 1879 by means of a metal stud marked 'VR 254', the number for Reading. (Bottom left) Mochaware pint, Swansea Pottery, c.1850. (Bottom right) Modern heavy glass mug, made in Italy.*

ACKNOWLEDGEMENTS
I am indebted to the work of Professor R. D. Connor and Carl Ricketts. Without their scholarly research the backbone of this story could never have been formed. Many people – dealers, fellow collectors, museum staff and trading standards officers – have helped me with information and material for illustration. I would like to thank them all, and in particular Jonathan Horne, Derek Harper and Carl Ricketts, for permission to use photographs from their collections. Illustrations are acknowledged as follows: Brighton and Hove Museums, page 21 (bottom left); British Museum Collection (drawings by Isabel Rock), page 18 (all); Bury Trading Standards, pages 55 (both), 56 (all), 57 (top two); Derby Museum and Art Gallery, page 6; Doncaster Museum Service, Doncaster MBC, pages 23 (centre), 27 (top two); Chris Green, page 22 (top); Derek Harper, pages 14, 29 (all), 35 (bottom two); Jonathan Horne, pages 19 (top two), 20 (all), 21 (bottom right), front cover (top left); Mrs Hornsby, pages 10 (both), 38 (upper), 58 (top); Ian Howes, page 37; *Illustrated London News*, page 27 (bottom); the Lacquer Chest, London, page 33 (top two); Museum of London, page 19 (lower); National Museum of Wales, page 25 (bottom two); Robert Opie, page 50 (bottom left); Penlee House Museum and Gallery, Penzance, page 34 (all); the Potteries Museum and Art Gallery, Stoke-on-Trent, pages 21 (top), 23 (top), 25 (upper), 28 (top two), 30 (top left), 31 (centre three and bottom); Public Record Office, pages 52 (top left and bottom right); Carl Ricketts, pages 7, 8, 9, 38 (bottom), 39 (both); drawing by Isabel Rock, page 23 (bottom); Winchester Museums Service, pages 5, 11 (all), 16; Trevor Wood, page 45 (top); the Worshipful Company of Pewterers, page 41 (top). All others are from the author's own collection.

Printed in Malta by Gutenberg Press Limited, Gudja Road, Tarxien PLA 19, Malta.

Contents

A mochaware quart and pint badged for the Queen's Arms, Goring, Oxfordshire; marked 'ER71'; Maling, 1901–10. This pair with high-quality decoration would have been specially selected stock for the customer's order.

Introduction

There are countless beer mugs for the collector to choose from but only a small fraction of these bear the official marks that show they were used in a public house, thus making them the subject of this book.

The marks on mugs are often mistakenly called excise marks, but there was no duty involved and they are really a guaranteed pint mark applied by the local authority. A 'pint' has not always been the pint that we know today. The possibility of deception was compounded by a number of local measures and different official standard pints. Behind the dry phrases of Acts of Parliament lies a lively skirmish with short measure. This book first looks at the history of the pint itself and the legislation controlling public house mugs, before going on to discuss materials and styles. In medieval times beer was often served in wooden mazers or leather pitchers, but too few of these mugs survive to form any useful picture, so we concentrate here on earthenware, pewter and glass.

Public house mugs have never been considered as a class, but they should be because special requirements brought about a particular style. As articles of trade they were subject to the strictest economy of production. The potter nevertheless had to produce something attractive enough to appeal. The publican, concerned with pilferage, favoured a style distinct from the domestic. These factors explain the resounding success of mochaware, which from beginnings around the end of the eighteenth century rapidly became the style of choice for a hundred years and produced a unique British style unknown on the Continent.

The story of beer mugs has been hidden from history. They are only a small part of the history of ceramics and glass and publications on these crafts give precedence to more showy examples. Mugs were utility items, sold by the gross to publicans with no sentimental attachment to their stock, and were used until smashed. That any survive at all must be due to their liberation from the pub to the home, where they retire to more peaceful service as holders for pencils, drill bits and flowers. This book aims to bring out the history that these remnants represent.

Note on terminology: I have tended to avoid using the words 'tavern', 'ale' and 'tankard' in the belief that these are today no more than romantic synonyms for 'pub', 'beer' and 'mug'.

The origins of the pint

The pint is ultimately derived from a wagon-load of grain. This may seem rather vague, but we can appreciate that a customary optimum size of ox cart would have evolved over the years, neither too small to be wasteful of journeys, nor too large to be exhausting for the animals, and related to the construction materials of the time. This size remained unchanged for centuries. Similarly today we have 40 foot (12 metre) articulated lorries containing twenty-six pallets, which is the standard lorry-load of commerce. The cartload was called a 'wey', which is a variant of the word 'weigh', showing that transport, weight and load are related ideas.

We can estimate this cartload as a little over one ton (about 1000 kg or 2200 pounds). For grain this was divided into quarters, a quarter of barley being a convenient quantity from which a brewer could make a few barrels of beer. The quarter

Exchequer gallon of Henry VII, 1497, made in heavy cast bronze, inscribed 'Henricus Septimus' with the Tudor badge of a rose, greyhound and portcullis. This is the earliest surviving government standard measure. Forty-two sets were issued to the most important towns and ports. Standards for weights and measures are a primary function of government and were vital in protecting its revenue as the duty on a gallon of wine cannot be collected if the measure cannot be defined.

was then divided into 8 bushels, a bushel being a convenient measure of wheat to keep a family in bread for a week. The bushel in turn divides into 8 gallons, each of 8 pints. Readers may by now have calculated that one cartload equals 2048 pints and recognise this as a sequence of binary divisions, which means only a naturally convenient method of distributing goods by cutting each portion into half, as distinct from the decimal metric system of cutting into ten.

The equivalent calculation can be done for liquid. French wine was exported in a tun of 256 gallons, which formed a European unit of trade. This travelled through Bruges and its port of Damme, where the French wine staple controlled the measures. The tun gives 256 x 8 = 2048 pints. The combination of these wet and dry systems is found in the earliest known official definition of capacity measure, the *Tractatus de Ponderibus et Mensuris*, usually attributed to Henry III, 1266: 'eight pounds make a gallon of wine and eight gallons make a bushel of London; which is the eighth part of a quarter.'

We have, however, made a gross oversimplification in our calculations. In practice no less than six standard gallons were

Standard pint of Elizabeth I, made in heavy cast bronze, together with its original leather carrying case; issued to the city of Derby in 1601.

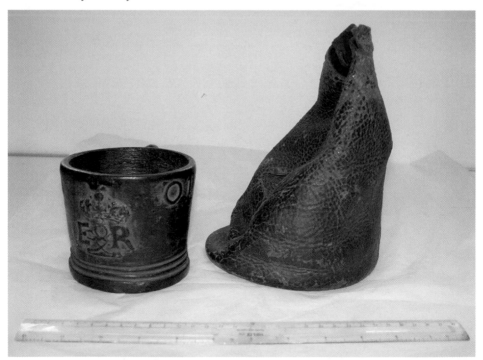

An Irish capacity pint in pewter by Charles Clarke of Waterford, c.1800. This is about four-fifths of the English pint, despite being certified with a GR and crown. The Irish Act of 1495 deemed all English statutes to apply to Ireland, but the old gallon was retained instead of Henry VII's new standard. In 1695 the Irish parliament confirmed the use of the Henry VII gallon but by another quirk in the law this was taken as applying to grain measures only!

in use in England and Scotland during the fourteenth century. The history of the pint is tortuously complicated by several factors. Four different pounds were in use to define weight: avoirdupois, troy, the Tower and Paris pounds. Different standards were in use for wine, ale and corn. The use of heaped or stricken measure (grain struck level with the top of the container using a stick) and customary allowances for spillage could add extra to a measure. Old English practice is mixed with French and Norman influence. Gallons could be based on 8 or 12 pounds and divided into 6 or 8 pints.

The six standard gallons together with the pints and quarts derived from them are summarised in Appendix 1. The only distinction that needs to be noted here is the completely different pints for wine measure and ale measure.

Physical standards of many of these measures can be seen today in museums. The Stirling jug, the foundation of Scottish measures, can be seen at Stirling Castle Museum and many town museums have interesting sets of standard measures once issued by central government.

It was intended that this multiple system would be cleared away by the milestone Weights and Measures Act (1824). This introduced the imperial gallon, defined as the volume of the weight of 10 pounds (160 ounces) of water. This gave a new pint of 20 ounces, two per cent short of the ale pint. The actual pint that we use today is therefore of relatively recent origin.

The British pint is the sole survivor of an ancient system of liquid measures that was replaced by the move to metrication in the 1970s. This formed a complete series of measures consisting of the gallon, half gallon, quart, pint, half pint, gill, half gill and quarter gill, which gave convenient sizes for the measurement of all liquids from milk to spirits.

A Scottish pewter chopin, about one and a half English pints, together with a half mutchkin, a quarter of a chopin, c.1760. The Scottish measures were based on the Stirling jug of nearly three pints. This dates from around 1500 and is kept at Stirling Castle. Not much notice was taken of the Act of Union (1705), applying English measures to Scotland, and Scottish measures are found as late as 1880.

Along with the physical artefacts some colourful names have been lost, such as the noggin, a quarter pint, now replaced by the 125 ml glass; the dram, a quarter gill, now replaced by the 25 ml shot; and the pottle, half a gallon.

The reference standard for the pint has also been abolished. The pound, which defined the gallon, is no longer recognised, so the pint is now defined by the National Weights and Measures laboratory by reference to the metric system – 568 millilitres. Although legal for trade, the use of the pint is circumscribed and restricted to the serving of draft beer and cider only. The Capacity Serving Regulations SI No. 20 1988 permits the serving of draft beer and cider only in measures of one third of a pint, half a pint or multiples of half a pint. No other fractions of a pint or other units related to the gallon are allowed. Although many pubs serve jugs of beer or mixers it would not be legal for these to be described as a quart or half gallon, only as 2 or 4 pints. It would not be legal to sell a half pint of wine! The publican serves his beer by the pint but has to order it by the litre and the brewery pays excise by the litre. This

A pewter wine pint of the Queen Anne standard, four-fifths the quantity of an ale pint; made in Bristol.

delightfully hybrid arrangement, which most people happily accept without a conscious thought, does go to prove how needless is the bureaucratic urge to uniformity.

The survival of the pint is usually attributed to sentimental attachment, but a more compelling reason is the accident that the nearest metric equivalent of the pint is smaller, 500 ml against 568 ml. This was a situation reversed in the case of the pound, 500 grams against 454 grams. This led to concerted opposition from both trade and consumer groups. The publicans and brewers were fearful of a drop in volume as everyone drank the smaller measure (a proposition which if true would provide a wonderful means for government control of excessive drinking). Consumers were outraged at the likelihood of being charged the same price for the smaller measure as for the larger. In the face of this storm the government wilted, much to the disappointment of the Metrication Board. Happily the rising tide of metrication has receded for the time being and the collector retains a live link to the past. It is still possible to add excellent examples of modern pint designs.

Although you can still buy a 'pint' of beer in the United States of America you will be short changed by 20 per cent. The American measures are based on the Queen Anne wine gallon, inherited from colonial times. The USA was an independent state in 1824, when Britain's Weights and Measures Act was passed, and so took no notice of the introduction of the imperial standard in Britain.

The quest for a fair pint

We take for granted today the fairness and convenience of being able to buy a standard pint in any pub in the United Kingdom. We are also used to legislation meaning what it says and being uniformly applied, but none of this was true in relation to the pint for a period of two hundred years from 1699.

Actual practice was quite different from what we would imagine from reading the legislation. Many obstacles were placed in the path of Parliament's badly expressed intentions. Attempts to change accepted and familiar weights and measures are inevitably stalled by inertia. There were a large number of enforcement authorities with jealously guarded rights and varying degrees of competence. Legislative clauses could be defeated by the interpretation of magistrates. There were practical difficulties in the methods and expense of marking mugs. All these factors provided plenty of opportunity for 'short measure'.

There was resistance from the trade, but we should have some sympathy for the publican. From time immemorial the retail price of beer, and of that other staple food, bread, has been controlled by government with its own interests in mind rather than the practicalities of making a living from selling beer, with its ever present risk of spoilt brews and poor malt. The Assize of Bread and Ale for 1266 stated: 'when a quarter of malt is sold for 20 pence then brewers in cities ought and may well afford to sell 2 gallons of beer for a penny and out of cities to sell 3 or 4 gallons for a penny.' A statute of James I set a penny as the price

'Pennyworth measures' made in pewter, c.1830 and 1890. These were convenient units of purchase for many customers but do not relate to any standard size. Legal cases upholding the validity of this 'contract by price' undermined the legislation requiring sales to be by imperial measure only.

False measure! These stoneware quarts are a good wineglass short of the full ale quart, despite being certified by the potter with a GR and crown stamp (985 ml and 950 ml against 1156 ml). The customer would stand no chance of assessing this by appearance. Lashford could have argued that his mug was intended for use only as a wine measure, with which it accords exactly, but there was never any requirement to stamp these and the situation shows the added potential for fraud with dual systems of measurement in use. Daniel Lashford and Richard Lamb are recorded as licensed victuallers in the city of Winchester around 1745. The mugs were found in a well in 1988.

for one quart of best ale or two quarts of small ale (small ale is the equivalent of reusing the teabag to make a second and third cup of tea). Regulations were detailed, different prices being set for 'on' and 'off' sales, innkeepers and victuallers (the early distinction between hotels and pubs). Publicans could always be found breaking the assize and some are recorded as paying a yearly fine to avoid endless appearances in court. Penalties otherwise were severe: 'if he sell not after the price of malt he is to be fined 12 pence the first time, 20 pence the second time and for the third time he is to be judged in the cukkingstole and afterwards put in the pillory.'

The foundation of pint marking for pubs is the Act for Ascertaining the Measures for Retailing Ale and Beer 1699, 11 and 12 William III. This Act complained that the innkeepers' practice of selling beer and ale in uncertain measures, much less than the standard, was reducing the consumption of malted liquor and lessening the King's excise revenues. It therefore commanded all innkeepers to sell beer and ale by the standard ale pint in vessels equalled to the standards and marked as such with a crown and the royal cipher 'WR'. It provided for the mayor or chief officer of each city or borough to effect the sizing and stamping at a charge of one farthing per vessel, using brass standard vessels to be issued from the Exchequer by the collectors of excise. This would appear quite clear-cut and one might wonder why two more centuries of legislation were needed to achieve the stated purpose of this Act. On investigation, however, many uncertainties appear.

We have already noted the existence of parallel measuring systems for wine and beer. Any publican, therefore, from then on would have had to keep two separate sets of mugs: one for ale and beer, the other for port, sherry and strong liquors. (Nothing is known of the correct measure for cider.) Confusion was likely to occur. The law did not require the vessel to be stamped with the particular pint it represented and there are surviving examples of pewter mugs bearing the wine pint size, the Irish pint or the Scottish mutchkin, all well short of the ale pint, but all bearing the crown and WR.

In providing for the mayor of each town to arrange for the stamping of vessels, Parliament had thrown an immense task on the elementary organisation of trading regulation. It was one thing for the clerk of the market to be present with a standard bushel for the use of the public, but quite another to stamp every beer mug in the county. We gain some idea of the scale of operation involved from Charles Stock, Inspector of Weights and Measures for the Brewer Street station in Middlesex. Giving evidence to the 1835 Select Committee, he described how he employed twenty staff dealing with one or two hundred people a day bringing items for verification. At the date of making up his return he had examined 96,000 items, among which were 33,445 pints and 15,450 quarts approved plus 2882 pints and 1998 quarts rejected. Even so, he estimated that one-fifth of all weights and measures in his district remained unverified.

A multitude of bodies was responsible for the local administration of this Act, and both the interpretation and the application were bound to vary widely. The shires were divided into approximately 900 hundreds, each with a court presided over by a sheriff or bailiff. There were also towns, boroughs and corporations (246 municipal boroughs in 1833). In addition to these there were many 'franchises', manors, lordships, liberties and universities that by ancient right exercised jurisdiction over weights and measures and gained income thereby. The universities of Oxford and Cambridge were specifically exempted from the operation of the Act, students being presumably considered fair game to be cheated. These bodies could not necessarily be relied upon to keep within the law themselves. Many of them are recorded as never having obtained an official set of standards, and in 1869 Mr Chisholm, the Warden of the Standards, listed sixty-seven districts of inspection that had not sent in their annual return and twelve counties and ninety-eight boroughs that had not submitted their standards for the compulsory five-yearly re-verification.

A magistrates' notice in the *Daily Advertiser* of 4th January 1754 shows both the law falling into abeyance and the magistrates' own misinterpretation of its requirements: 'There

NOTICE

Whereas by the Laws and Statutes of This Realm

16 99

IS HEREBY GIVEN TO ALL

INN KEEPERS, ALEHOUSE KEEPERS, SUTLERS, VICTUALLERS

and other Retailers of

ALE and BEER

AND EVERY OTHER PERSON or PERSONS KEEPING A PUBLIC HOUSE
IN ANY
CITY, TOWN CORPORATE, BOROUGH, MARKET TOWN, VILLAGE, HAMLET, PARISH,
PART or PLACE IN THE Kingdom of England

That, as from the 24th day of JUNE 1700

THEY SHALL BE REQUIRED TO RETAIL and SELL THEIR ALE & BEER

by the **FULL ALE QUART** OR **PINT**

According to the Laid Standard

IN VESSELS DULY MARKED with W.R and CROWN
be they made of

WOOD, GLASS, HORN, LEATHER OR PEWTER etc.

Any Person Retailing Ale or Beer to a TRAVELLER or WAYFARER in Vessels not
signed and marked as aforesaid will be liable to a **PENALTY** not exceeding

FORTY SHILLINGS

FOR EVERY SUCH OFFENCE

By Act of Parliament ~ at WESTMINSTER
In the Reign of Our Sovereign ~ WILLIAM III by the Grace of God, King,
Defender of the Faith &c

Notice giving effect to the Act for Ascertaining the Measures for Retailing Ale and Beer. Although there were earlier attempts to establish verification of mugs, such as that of the Lord Mayor of London in 1423, this was the first nationwide measure to ensure that all public house mugs were stamped.

has not been any pots stamped (unless counterfeitly done) for many years past. Notice is hereby given that a method will be put into execution (to effect the law). Note all pots whereby wine or other strong liquors are rendered are likewise by Act of Parliament obliged to be stamped.' There was never any requirement to stamp a wine measure, nor any device that would have distinguished it from an ale measure.

Practical difficulties arising from the stamping of pots defeat the expectation of local verification. While pewter can easily be stamped, earthenware can be indelibly marked only before firing. This necessarily meant that responsibility for marking devolved upon the potter. Mugs with potter-applied stamps have been found from the major stoneware-producing areas of London, Bristol, Nottingham and Staffordshire. The geographical spread of finds shows that they were distributed over a wide area. The law was complied with to some extent with immediate effect, but neither northern potteries nor locally produced earthenware figure among surviving examples and it is thought that large parts of Britain may have ignored the new provisions. Whether there was supervision from the local authority we do not know, but even these 'official' mugs show a bias towards short measure. Examination of vessels excavated at John Dwight's Fulham pottery show an average 5 per cent discrepancy, with some pots 10 per cent under size. We can also imagine that any kind-hearted potter who deliberately oversized his pots to ensure a good measure would soon lose the business of his trade customers.

Marking of glass is also problematic. It would be possible to impress a mark while the glass was hot, but no example has been found. The engraving of a mark would not be within the

Local and customary measures! The mochaware mug on the left is one third of a quart, shown with a pint for comparison. The small size is too obvious to be used for intentional deceit. It would more likely be the only size that could be had in a town where short measure was prevalent. It might also be used to serve customers in the saloon, charged as a pint, by way of the landlord recouping the expense of providing comfortable surroundings.

competence or farthing budget of the local official. The soldering of a pewter tag round the base or handle has the same objection. Although glass is mentioned in the 1699 Act, no marked examples dating before 1878 have been found.

There was resistance to the ale pint on account of regional attachment to local and customary measures. Many of these involved natural but non-standard fractions of a pint. A 'can' was common in Bristol, being one third of a quart, 13.3 fluid ounces. In Shrewsbury a 'quart' was traditionally one and a half pints. In Salisbury a pint was divided into *thrœ* half-pints, each of only 6.7 ounces. An 18 ounce pint has been commonly seen in pewter mugs from Newcastle, Birmingham and Warrington. The Irish pint was about four-fifths of the ale pint, and although the ale pint was supposedly adopted in 1695 the Irish pint remained in use until the arrival of imperial measure. The Act of Union of the Scottish and English parliaments in 1707 specified that Scottish measures should be the same as English, but Scottish mutchkins of 13.75 ounces capacity continued in use.

The 'contract by price' could justify measures of any size, bearing no relation to any standard unit. It was a common service to customers to sell beer (and many other items) by the pennyworth or three pence worth. Publicans would have a special container made for this purpose. While some prosecutions for this practice have been recorded, the case of Craig v McPhee in the 1883 court session in Glasgow established its lawfulness on the grounds that the measures were not represented to the customer as containing any particular quantity.

Parliament did nothing to clear up this swarm of odd sizes; indeed, its Acts are remarkable for self-contradiction on the subject. The milestone 1824 Weights and Measures Act, which introduced the imperial system, purported to set one standard throughout the United Kingdom, but at the same time it allowed for local measures lawfully to continue in use, provided that they were marked with the ratio that they bore to imperial measure – a most unlikely event. No earthenware has been found so marked but pewter mugs have been found stamped '5/6 IS' (imperial standard) and '31/32'. As the old ale pint was 2 per cent larger than the new imperial one there was little objection to continued use of existing mugs.

By 1834 there was almost no protection against the serving of short measure. This was the opinion of Mr Gingell, Inspector for Weights and Measures for Bristol, in his evidence to the Commission on the Restoration of the Standards (which had been destroyed in the fire at the House of Commons):

'The law is a combination of disjunctions; no two lawyers can be found to agree on any one of its clauses... The 5th and 6th William IV (1835) abolishes all customary measures and enacts that every person who shall sell by any denomination of measure other than Imperial shall forfeit the sum of 40 shillings, yet in the latter part of the same section it provides that you may sell by any measure you please if you will not call it Imperial. This upsets the whole system, so that neither magistrate nor inspector can safely act under this section. The public are aware of this and it is quite unsafe to press a conviction. Earthenware cups are almost exclusively used in this city for short measure, the landlords preferring them as they can get any size they please, making short measure proverbial here. A variety of measures are used, by the names can, tankard, jug, nip, mug etc, which are all short of Imperial yet charged as such. Licensed victuallers, when a pint or quart is requested, if they suspect a person say "We don't draw full measure in this room, if you want full measure you must go to the tap room." Thus a decent man is shut out of the parlour unless he submits to short measure.'

It was not until the Weights and Measures Act of 1879 that comprehensive marking was introduced. The concentration of glass and earthenware manufacture into large industries and the simple method of sand-blasting a mark on to glass or pottery made the marking of every mug a feasible proposition. Salaried inspectors could be appointed and a system of unified stamp numbers to identify local authorities was introduced. Under the 1892 Weights and Measures (Purchase) Act councils were able to acquire the franchises of ancient bodies and the administration began to take on the form that we know today.

Standard quart and pint of William III made in heavy cast bronze, issued to the city of Winchester in 1700. These standards were sent out by the Commissioners for Excise to many local authorities as one of the requirements of the Act for Ascertaining the Measures for Retailing Ale and Beer.

There has been controversy for four hundred years over the simple question of the froth in the head of the beer. Does it constitute part of the measure, or should customers receive a full liquid pint? John Powell, a clerk of the market in the time of Elizabeth I, and whose treatise on measures has come down to us, recommended the use of the *thurdendel*. This was a vessel slightly larger than a quart that allowed room for the froth as well as a full quart of liquid. This is the origin of the line measure. In official terminology pint mugs are 'capacity serving measures' of two sorts, either 'brim measure' or 'line measure', that is they are a measure and a serving glass combined into one. In the brim measure the brim itself defines the capacity, whereas in the line measure this is done by the line placed just short of the brim.

Many examples of line measures can be found today; some of the best, with lines incorporated in the mould, can be found among 1960s keg mugs. However, the line measure for beer has never found acceptance in the trade, despite being an excellent way to prevent beer spillage on carpets. This contrasts with universal acceptance of line measures for serving wine.

Investigation by CAMRA (the Campaign for Real Ale) shows that 80 per cent of pubs serve less than 100 per cent liquid and that one in five pints are more than 5 per cent deficient. The law on the subject is clear. Section 19 of the Weights and Measures Act 1979 states: 'in ascertaining the quantity of any beer... the gas comprised in any foam shall be disregarded.' This section, however, was never implemented. Magistrates have upheld the view that the head is part of the measure because customers expect a head and because it is legal to use brim measures but also completely impossible to use them to serve a full liquid pint unless the beer is flat, concluding that the head must legally be included as part of the pint.

These decisions have made it impossible for inspectors to take action against the serving of short pints. To echo Mr Gingell in 1835, 'it is quite unsafe to press for a conviction'. In an effort to remedy the situation, Dennis Turner MP introduced a Private Members' Bill in 1997 but this fell at the report stage. A Department of Trade and Industry consultation paper on draught beer measures in 2001 recommended use of the average system as is done for all other food and drink packaging, but this has never been put into effect, the government being strongly in favour of a 'self-regulatory solution to the issue of serving a fair measure of beer'.

To our amusement, it is likely as ever that you will be served a short pint, the only difference today being that it will at last invariably be provided in an officially verified mug!

Stoneware

Stoneware was the aristocrat of European pottery from its conception in Germany around 1200 until the burst of ceramic invention in the eighteenth century made it look old-fashioned and relegated it to utility ware. The material was ideally suited to beer mugs. Made from clay mixed with ground calcined flint, it was strong and completely impervious to liquids because of its vitrification at 1300 degrees centigrade, a temperature not possible without a special kiln. It was easy to make attractive. The colour of the fabric varied with the different clays through all shades of brown. Two-tone effects could be given by dipping in a different-coloured slip (liquid clay) and the salt glaze formed a mottled orange-peel effect sometimes referred to as 'tiger-skin'.

So much appreciated was the ware that the industries in Siegburg, Frechen, Westerwald

Left: *Globular mug with a medallion 'W E Barrett in Handyard in Holborn London 1668'. This mug of German origin testifies to the good representation in London of the Rhine stoneware industry and the execution of special orders.*

Below: *Mugs from Westerwald bearing crowned AR and GR medallions, specially made for the English pub trade; salt-glazed light grey stoneware with cobalt blue decoration. Note the tapered rim suitable for the optional fitting of a pewter mount or lid.*

Above left and right: *Gorge with lathe-turned decoration to the neck and WR and crown stamp at the base of the handle; c.1700, London, possibly by John Dwight.*

Right: *The earliest dated London tavern mug, inscribed 'John Clifford att the goate White Cross Street 1708'; stamped with AR and crown.*

and other districts around Cologne developed an international trade. The port books of Exeter for 1636 show 1200 casts being landed (a cast being a variable number of pots made from a fixed weight of clay, taken as three pots for customs purposes).

The success of John Dwight's experiments at Fulham, with the grant of his patent in 1671, soon led to a flourishing English industry. Notable producers were James Stiff, Doulton & Watts at Lambeth, the Vauxhall and Mortlake potteries, William Powell in Bristol, John Morley in Nottingham, and many others in Burslem, Derbyshire and Liverpool.

Stoneware pint mug with AR and crown stamp beneath the handle. Typical London style and fine quality with a Britannia medallion and silver mount to the rim; c.1705.

There was an evolution of style in mugs. Early examples followed the Germanic form of a globular mug with a narrow neck known as a gorge. The straight-sided cylinder soon appeared and became the dominant form, known as the London style. Attractive features of stoneware are applied moulded pub signs, and the names of landlords, pubs and towns.

Stoneware cylindrical mugs, which began to supersede the globular style. (Left) Pint mug stamped with WR and crown, with lathe-turned foot and distinctive early ear-shape handle; found in the 1930s during alterations to the Crown Staffordshire china factory. (Right) Quart mug stamped with AR and crown beneath the handle, and with silver mount inscribed 1704; typical Nottingham style.

Staffordshire brown stoneware mugs, c.1710, excavated from the site of the George Inn at Burslem, verified with a crown and AR stamp. The buff grey body was dipped in an iron wash, salt-glazed and decorated in a manner known as scratchware, a term that elevates to a technique the most elementary way to decorate a pot, and which is done with varying degrees of success. The design here is known as a 'tulip'.

Above left: Quart stoneware mug with WR stamp; decorated with an applied inn sign of The Gun; impressed 'Thos Furner Brighelmstone [Brighton] 1766'; thought to have been made in Bristol.

Above right: Salt-glazed stoneware quart mug with WR and crown stamp to the top left of the handle; also impressed NO – possibly the work of Nathaniel Oade, who is recorded as taking over the Gravel Lane works at Southwark; found by the Kent Archaeological Rescue Unit in a well in the back garden of the Crown and Anchor tavern in Woolwich.

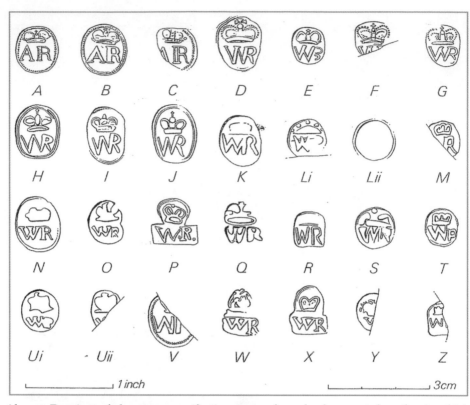

Above: *Drawings of ale measure verification stamps from shards excavated on the site of John Dwight's Fulham pottery. Careful comparison with these stamps has allowed some mugs to be*

attributed to Dwight's pottery. Verification marks on pub mugs are a huge help in identifying dates and manufacturers throughout the three hundred years that they have been a requirement.

The relative importance of stoneware for beer mugs must be kept in perspective. It was expensive, generally three or four times the price of local ware owing to the cost of transport for the flint and the finished pot. It is unlikely ever to have accounted for more than a minority of the overall market, which was well served by local potters using friable local clays and

Waisted mug. This style is a larger version of the capuchin, popular for drinking coffee and chocolate, c.1750; indistinct mark; lead glaze over orange-brown dip.

Two Staffordshire mugs, c.1580, made with friable local clay and given an iron-rich lead glaze to render them suitable for holding liquid. Indigenous pottery, produced throughout Britain, was the poor relation of imported German stoneware but was cheap to produce and served the bulk of the market.

Above and left: Staffordshire 'scratch blue'. Curved and straight pints and a half pint with GR and crown medallions. White stoneware made with crushed calcined flints and Devon white clay imported via Liverpool. The decorators of this ware were called 'flowerers'. Note the cursory workmanship. Judging from the number of survivals, this was a popular range of pubware in the period 1740–80.

Left and above: *An ugly mug! Earthenware in stoneware style from a very worn mould, with barely discernible relief figures and pint impression. This was produced in large numbers by Kilnhurst Pottery in South Yorkshire and known as 'Bristol ware' on account of the original location of the factory. This example dates from before 1879. Later examples can be found stamped 'VR37', the verification number for Sheffield.*

iron or manganese glaze. These local products included wares known variously as black ware, treacle ware, Midlands yellow ware and Cistercian ware (because of its prevalence in monastic excavations). It is safe to say that wherever there was a pottery beer mugs were being made. Serving their purpose but undistinguished by ornament, these items have disappeared from the record almost completely, leaving stoneware prominent among exhibits in museums.

Though superseded, stoneware had perennial appeal and Doulton continued to produce it. The half pint here is crisply decorated; verified 'VR67', c.1890. The pint is marked GR, c.1910–52. The Lambeth factory closed in 1956.

Mochaware

Mochaware is given short mention in ceramic reference books, but for the beer-mug collector it is a major subject because of its central importance in the history of mugs and because of its potential to form a colourful display.

Mochaware is a decorative variant of creamware, a new earthenware body perfected by Wedgwood in about 1760. The smooth body of this ware made possible many attractive new styles for which the pitted surface of salt-glazed stoneware was not ideal, including transfer printing and spongeware (colour dabbed on with a sponge). Mochaware is a decorative method normally associated with a style known as banded slipware. This is produced by dipping the plain body in slip, which was then allowed to dry. The piece was then turned in a lathe to expose parts of the underlying body, giving rings of different colour. These rings in turn could be coloured with contrasting dark slip added on the lathe. This sounds complicated but in the hands of a

Left: *A Staffordshire red earthenware mug given a manganese glaze, with an AR and crown applied as a moulded pad; c.1701. This mug is of interest as an early example of this style of marking, later to be adopted on mochaware.*

Below: *A pearlware mug verified with a metal tag fixed to the handle, the earliest known example of this method being used, c.1760.*

An early mochaware pint mug with bold banding and turned foot. The sprig is moulded 'WRIV IMPERIAL'. This is one of the earliest known sprigs on mochaware and dates to 1830–7. These sprigs fulfilled the legal requirement for marking in a way more decorative than the plain impressed marks on stoneware.

skilled worker it is an astonishingly quick way to produce an attractive banded mug.

Mochaware is characterised by tree- or fern-like patterns that were produced by the reaction of a spot of acid 'tea' applied to the wet slip. It was an economical means of producing an individual design without the need for skilled painting and so was suited to the production of utilitarian wares. The name comes from the similarity to Mocha stone, a form of moss agate that when cut and polished displays crystalline patterns of fern-like form, the best of which were exported from the Red Sea port of Mocha in Yemen. Noel Teulon-Porter, an early collector, believed that drinkers knew it only as tree, moss, seaweed or fern pottery. It was prevalent enough for a man who had been drinking to say, euphemistically, that he had been out 'lifting trees'.

The heyday of mochaware was the second half of the nineteenth century. To judge by the ratio of surviving pieces, mochaware was much more popular than glass in the pint and quart sizes. Many pubs must have used mochaware exclusively for their service in the larger sizes and it would have presented a colourful scene that today we find difficult to visualise, being completely unused to earthenware in pubs.

Mochaware is considered a purely English invention. It is known to have been produced in Staffordshire by the Adams family around 1785 and the earliest dated piece is 1789. The

Shard excavated from the site of the Don Pottery, which allowed the William IV mug on page 26 to be identified. 'VRI' stands for 'Victoria Regina Imperatrix'. The title was conferred by Parliament in 1875 and gives us a close date for the shard.

firm that the collector is most likely to come across is C. T. Maling of Newcastle, whose prodigious output, for the whole of the nineteenth century and up to the First World War, is reflected in the high proportion of their pieces still available today. Although it is rare for any piece to be marked with the maker's name, we are able to identify some makers from the local authority verification numbers introduced in 1879, in Maling's case 71 for Newcastle. Stylistic similarities can then be related to earlier pieces. Maling had a particular house style of three double bands of thin black banding, some distinctive

A quart mochaware mug in use, with more mugs displayed on the bar shelves, c.1910. Pictures of earthenware in pubs are few and the paucity of the record belies the popularity of the ware and the widespread industry supported by the demand. Today's supply of pub glasses is 60 million per annum. If we accept that this must equal the rate of breakage, just over one per person per year, then a mountain of mugs has been produced and smashed over three hundred years.

Early Victorian mochaware pints and a quart with soldered metal bands round the base stamped 'PINT' and 'QUART' (too faint to show in the photograph). These bands are a puzzle as they do not bear official marks. The likely explanation is that in the period after 1835, when earthenware was exempt from official verification, the law was nevertheless interpreted as requiring the capacity to be stated. Application of these bands would allow publicans to use ware from potters not specifically geared to the pub trade and therefore marking their pots at manufacture. This is consistent with the individual style of these mugs compared to the semi-standardisation of the regular trade.

shapes including mugs with a turned base, and an attractive green and blue colour combination. Between 1824 and 1879 pieces are found with applied moulded sprigs indicating pint, quart and imperial standard.

Other prominent manufacturers were T. G. Green of Church Gresley in Derbyshire, Edge Malkin and John Tams in Staffordshire, the Llanelli and Swansea potteries in South

A group of early Victorian mochaware, c.1840–80. Blue and green was a favourite colour scheme with various manufacturers. (Centre) Half pint with sprig identified as Staffordshire. Half pints are not frequent in mochaware as the size was catered for by glass. (Left) Pint with rubber ink stamp underglaze. (Right) Quart: this has a copper stud through the wall of the pot, stamped 'VR254', a re-verification by Reading Borough with the reintroduction of marking requirements in 1879.

The quart shown here has been attributed to the Swansea Pottery from an identical waster dug up on site by Derek Harper. The cream and blue pint has been attributed on the basis of its identical sprig. Both are attractively produced, c.1862–70. Note the tapered shape of the quart and turned foot. South Wales produced some of the most attractive pub mugs. Although there was no good local clay, fuel and transport were readily available.

Above: A group of three pints from Llanelli Pottery. (Left) With ink-stamped imperial banner, also stamped to the side 'VR458'. This was the mark for Carmarthen district and the mug has been attributed to Llanelli as it was the only pottery in this area, c.1890. (Centre) Ink-stamped 'PINT', pre-1879. (Right) Stamped 'ER458', c.1901-10. Note the attractive deep blue.

Left: A pair of pints from an unidentified pottery in Swansea. Note the distinctive crown and riband, c.1860.

Above left: *A pint mug thought to be from Bovey Tracey, Devon, with characteristic absence of black banding.*

Above right: *Mochaware pint in attractive blue, marked 'ER19'; T. G. Green, Derbyshire, 1901–10.*

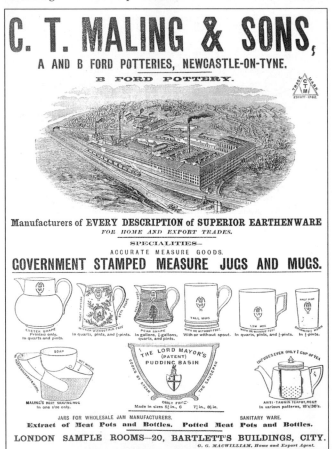

A trade advertisement of 1893 for Maling, a useful aid to identification.

Left and far left: An unusually squat-shaped mug with sprig and etched mark 'VR286'; South Wales, c.1879; possibly Dyfatty Street pottery, Swansea.

Mugs with transfer-printed capacity markings, applied under glaze by the potter at manufacture. The distinctive 'I.QUART' (imperial quart) design has been identified as Pountney of Bristol from an example in Bristol Museum.

Wales, Pountney, John Ellis and the Crown Pottery in Bristol, and the Don Pottery in Doncaster. The production was widespread and included firms not normally associated with this kind of pottery, such as Spode and Wedgwood, some of whose work is certainly represented in surviving mugs

A pair of mugs unusual for the horizontal position of the pattern; certified 'VR156'; Northampton, c.1880.

A selection of sprigs showing the individual nature of the designs. Some have been attributed to particular potters. A gathering of more evidence might well identify some of the others.

today but cannot be attributed.

The quality of mochaware varies widely and there is much for the collector to be selective about. Skill was needed to produce good tree patterns, but with finished pots selling at 10d per dozen speed was essential. Many trees are poorly defined and smudged; colours can be lively or drab; the placing of banding can be confident or half-hearted. The potteries were quite happy to sell their rejects; John Tams advertised that 'Crates of seconds can be had on application'. In addition to this, most of the surviving pieces are cracked, chipped or stained and so the collector must search hard to find good examples.

The quart was a popular size in mochaware, but nowadays it is not used at all. The evidence of the inspector Charles Stock

Left and far left: *The pattern of chevrons and dashes on this quart mug has been made using an embossed wheel impressed and rotated round the surface of the pot while the clay was still plastic. This technique, known as rouletting, produces an effective design in minimum time without skilled labour and is here used to pleasing effect, c.1840.*

Right and far right: *An unusually decorative transfer print from Davenport Pottery. The introduction of imperial measure would have been an occasion for potters to bring out new designs; William IV, 1830-7.*

Transfer-printed earthenware. (Left) Quart with oriental pagodas, marked 'ER19'; Derbyshire, 1901-10. (Right) Pint with English landscape marked with rubber inkstamp under glaze 'VR32'; Staffordshire, 1880-1901.

Transfer-printed ware. A lively hop design specially badged for the Alverne Inn, Penzance; stamped 'VR6'; Birmingham, 1880–1901. Coaney was a Birmingham firm well-known for pubware, including china spirit barrels.

quoted earlier shows a ratio of about one quart mug for every two pints and this ratio is reflected in the plentiful supply of quarts among surviving mochaware mugs. Why and when did this decline occur? The reasons can only be guessed at but it appears that it was not due to the beer becoming stronger. Statistics available from Customs and Excise show average specific gravity declining from 1055 in 1900 to 1041 in 1938. However, these figures hide a great decline in the consumption of mild beer and this perhaps provides a clue, for weak beer was often drunk as a safe alternative to water but was displaced by tea. It may be that people drank less as their jobs became

A late Victorian pint and half pint marked 'VR19', from an unidentified potter in Derbyshire. The hops and barley motif is identical on both sizes and can still be found on the same mug into the 1940s – great economy in design!

Below: *A blue and white transferware print depicting a lady on horseback in a rural scene, stamped 'VR71'; Maling, c.1890. An unusual find from Maling, so heavily associated with mochaware.*

Left. *A waisted mug that echoes the style of the eighteenth-century capuchin; marked 'half pint VR481'; Neath, c.1890. The transfer print is exactly the same as that of the preceding illustration. It is possible that the engraver sold the transfer to more than one customer or that the plates were sold to the Derbyshire potter. It is not unusual to find designs travelling in this way.*

Spongeware, with a neat transfer print 'IMPERIAL PINT'. Note the metal stud to the right of the handle. It was produced before 1879, then re-verified.

Plain glazed ware in cream with fine gilded lines; 'VR71', Maling, c.1890. Loving cups are difficult to relate to today. They are an attractive notion but we do not like other people drinking from our mug. Many loving cups are large decorative items that accord with our idea of symbolic function and occasional ceremonial use, but this is a utility item for everyday passing round the pub.

A 1930s echo of the waisted mug of 1700; marked 'GR 485', Hanley.

Beer mugs are always a jolly theme for decoration.

progressively less physical, but there must still be some cultural factor at work as the quart does effectively survive today in the one-litre steins of German beer halls. A definite answer remains elusive.

As to the timing, no quart glass mugs appear to have been made, so the decline must coincide with that of earthenware and it is safe to say that the quart was effectively dead by the end of the Second World War.

Pewter

The importance of pewter as a material for pub mugs has been exaggerated because of its indestructible nature and the abundant survival of Victorian examples. Though it was an excellent material for use in pubs there were disadvantages. The cost was ten times that of local earthenware and about three times that of Staffordshire stoneware. There was a constant risk of theft because of the ready cash value of the metal. Old pewter never dies; it is melted down to make new. The Oxford colleges record exchanging old pewter at about two-thirds the price of new. With tin at £3 10s per hundredweight in 1782 the $2^1/_4$ pounds of metal in a quart mug was worth 1s 6d, more than a day's wages for many workmen. In 1812 the Licensed Victuallers petitioned Parliament for protection against thefts by making it punishable to send out beer in pewter pots and to confine pewter to the measuring out of beer to customers. Their concern is explained by the fact that pubs offered a home delivery service. It was also common practice, as an inducement to loyalty, for the wholesaler of drink to provide mugs to the

Right: *Counter theft: a pewter mug engraved 'John Little at ye Horse and Jockey in Reading, if sold stole', 1690–9.*

Below: *A 'two-band' pewter pint with William and Mary verification and a 'high-band' quart made by John Harrison in York, c.1730.*

Bristol-made pewter mugs in 'droopy' style. Pint and quart of ale, standard capacity with a strap handle and hooded ball terminal, c.1730–40.

publican, who therefore had less of an interest in accounting for the return of mugs sent out. In these circumstances it would be an unusually well-to-do establishment that maintained all its service in pewter. In some other hostelries, such as coaching inns catering for rich travellers, it is likely that some pewter would be kept. Poorer establishments, lacking the refinement of stoneware, would have made use of local earthenware and might never have kept any pewter, except for a couple of measures.

Around 1740 pewter entered a period of steady decline. This

The tulip shape of pewter mug. The half pint with Liverpool verification, c.1840, and the pint with Bristol verification c.1800.

Class distinction in beer mugs. (Top) The gathering of gentlemen at the Charing Cross Inn, 1819, shows an array of pewter pots and tall flute glasses. (Left) A working men's pub in West Bromwich, 1850, after a boxing match, showing earthenware and two dram glasses. Samuel Pepys, attending the Lord Mayor's dinner in 1663, was most put out to be served in earthenware pitchers and wooden dishes.

coincided with the introduction of tea, which eventually replaced beer as basic refreshment and for which the heat-retaining property of china was preferred. In the second half of the century there were marvellous developments in pottery that produced attractive alternatives to pewter. The final blow to

A Cromwellian squat lidded pewter tankard, c.1650–60.

'old pewter' came from Britannia metal, originating in Sheffield around 1770. This type of pewter was made from an alloy of tin with antimony instead of the traditional lead or copper. It was a harder metal, produced in thin sheet that could be stamped with ornament and worked into fine light pieces with the elegant styles of silverware. These developments did not bear directly on the pub mug trade but the fall from favour in the home would have made the pubware look old-fashioned. In 1867 the Parish of St Pancras reported to the Standards Committee that they were stamping only a dozen pewter pots when fifteen years previously they would have stamped a gross.

The description of features on pewter mugs has a vocabulary of its own. The records of the Worshipful Company of Pewterers show that from early times there were many named styles of mugs, 'stope pots', 'tanggard pots', 'drinkyng cruses', 'hooped thurndells', 'barred pots' and 'Winchester pints', among many others. Unfortunately none of these names can be matched with the specimens that survive. We can, however, trace some evolution in form. In Stuart times the squat

A pot-bellied pewter quart inscribed 'Thos Mundy, Anchor, Basingstoke' and verified 'G IV TB C*S' (for George IV, Town of Basingstoke and County of Southampton), 1824–30.

lidded mug was dominant. The lids are a puzzle to us today. Were they just a passing fashion or were they a practical necessity to protect against the spitting of chewing tobacco and flying ash from long clay pipes? It has been suggested that they were a restraint of trade determined by the pewterers, there being more work and income in a lidded mug. Lids are cumbersome to use and they disappeared, never to be seen again. Early in the eighteenth century mugs became taller and narrower. Around 1820 the pot-bellied shape evolved and became the most popular form of the nineteenth century.

The craft of pewter making was organised in a tightly controlled guild. Manufacture was widely dispersed, with every town having a few pewterers, and regional preferences of style can be discerned. Of great interest to collectors is the fact that many of these individuals can be identified by the mark, known as a touch, that each applied to his work. Pewter mugs are also notable for the huge variety of town and borough verification marks that can be found. Carl Ricketts has identified over one thousand.

Glass

Some guesswork is needed to figure out the history of glass in pubs as there is a lengthy period for which we have no evidence. No marked pints pre-dating 1879 appear to have survived.

Although the Act of 1699 mentions glass it is probable that it was at the time neither economical nor sturdy enough for pub use. It is known from disputes over the monopoly in 1608 that 'forest glass' beakers suitable for beer were in production ('forest glass' was green glass, in distinction to the clear, thin, fragile and expensive Venetian 'cristallo' glass), but according to the price list of Sir Robert Mansell in 1624 these were 4s 6d per dozen, a price about five times that of earthenware. In the time of Elizabeth I and James I glass was considered an unnecessary luxury and probate inventories show that well-off households may have possessed glazed windows, a looking glass and a few bottles, but that drinking glasses were not

Very heavy early glass mugs, the pint weighing 1078 grams. This mug uses the possibilities of glass to show off an altogether larger than life pint. The nine-sided ribs act as magnifying lenses and there is a pronounced punt. This is the precursor to the later, slimmed-down, straight-sided mugs. Marked 'VR 324'; South Shields. Almost certainly by Edward Moore, c.1880.

The development of the straight-sided mug. These ten-sided designs are taller and narrower than the later version. (Left) 'GR 323', Gateshead, Sowerby or Davidsons. (Right) 'GR 64', Sunderland, Henry Greener, c.1910—30.

The winning straight-sided design of the 1930s: 'GR 478', Ravenhead Glass, St Helens.

The next most successful design of the 1930s: 'GR 323', Davidsons or Sowerby.

common. The new English lead glass invented by George Ravenscroft around 1680 was ideally suited to a sturdy style for pub use but the Glass Excise Act of 1745, in force for one hundred years, imposed a tax by weight and favoured lighter styles and higher value.

Conditions changed in the middle of the nineteenth century. Richardsons of Stourbridge imported American glass-moulding machines in 1833 and with the end of the tax in 1845 the pressed glass industry began to make glass articles of every description available to even the poorest households.

It is likely, however, that glass still did not make headway in pubs in face of the established usage of mochaware. Many examples of pressed glass pint mugs survive from this time but they are of the extravagantly decorated style indicating home use. Marked mugs after 1879 show that a typical plainer style was being

Above: *The most popular design of the 1930s, seen in action.*

The straight-sided mug chosen as a symbol by the brewers for press advertising, 1930.

Cylindrical mugs. (Left) With handsome foot and pronounced punt; 'VR 323', Gateshead, 1880—1900. (Right) With flared foot and rim, 'GR 323', Gateshead, c.1910—40.

used in pubs but the scarcity of these examples indicates lack of popularity.

A distinction must be made between the pint and the smaller sizes, which abound. A picture emerges, therefore, of earthenware and pewter predominant for pints and quarts and of glass used for the smaller sizes, where perhaps its versatility of form was an advantage.

At some stage during this period glass began its steady rise to the exclusive position it holds today. Charles Booth wrote in 1896: 'Until comparatively recently the publican's customers were very particular as to their ale being served in a nice bright pewter pot and the essential virtue of a potman was that he

Whiteways cider in an amber glass: 'GR 64', Sunderland, Henry Greener. A proprietary mould for this major cider producer. The amber glass is well suited to cider.

Heavy mugs in a proprietary design for Double Diamond. These are examples of excellent pint-to-line design with a ridged line moulded inside the rim.

should be a good pewter cleaner; the pot is, however, being now largely supplanted by glass.' The factors behind this are most likely to include the increase in interior lighting levels and the use of filtration to give clear drinks. Earthenware conveniently hid the cloudiness, sediment and floating bits that

The keg beer villains of the 1960s and 1970s, which provoked the Campaign for Real Ale. Marketing of national brands demanded the creation of a brand image, an important part of which was an exclusive proprietary mould.

The British are introduced to lager. 1960s keg pint-to-line mugs.

were the natural characteristic of all fermented drinks before the advent of modern filtration. The sparkle of glass is pre-eminent in showing off the appeal of a crystal-clear drink in good lighting conditions.

Glass goblets or rummers. (Left) Lettered 'HALF PINT' in relief moulding inside the bowl. (Centre) An attractive design with gadrooning to the bowl and baluster stem; moulded diamond registration mark internally, 10th September 1868, Ker Webb & Co, Manchester; verified 'VR310', Lancaster. (Right) Plain bowl relief-moulded 'Half pint patent VR 324'. This was an excellent way to mark glass but did not catch on. The patent cannot be traced but it is a South Shields manufacturer, c.1880.

The development of the dimple. (Left) Hexagonal flat facet design; 'GR 64', Sunderland, Henry Greener, 1920–40. (Centre) The classic dimple of the 1960s, this one marked '1966 478', Ravenhead Glass. (Right) Touched-up modern design produced by Dema, Chesterfield. (Inset) Once fashionable enough for advertising, as seen on this pub playing card, but now becoming history.

The candle-lit interiors of the eighteenth century were dark by modern standards of illumination. Gas lighting in the early part of the nineteenth century improved light levels but was initially weak and troublesome, and it was only with the development of the incandescent mantle in the 1880s that the brightness that we associate with gas was achieved. From the beginning of the twentieth century electric lighting brought greater brightness. Today lighting is an integral part of the design of

A modern rummer, a style now rarely met.

Victorian half-pint beer flutes. (Left) Lens-cut with hexagonal stem. (Centre) With light ribbing. (Right) Pressed glass with dimple pattern.

any new bar. The supreme position of modern glass has been reinforced by the invention of tempered borosilicate glass, giving unrivalled strength, design possibilities and hygiene.

Glass styles can be categorised under four headings: mugs,

Elegant beer drinking promoted by Double Diamond in a 1960s press advertisement. The glass was the most popular flute of the time, a modern descendant of dwarf ale glasses.

Modern flutes, light and elegant.

beakers, goblets and flutes. The term 'beaker' is revived here to replace the makeshift 'straight', which is a misnomer as the design of these elegant glasses is reliant on curves. 'Beaker' is precise in distinguishing a tall glass from a tumbler and is of

Glass beakers, the main alternative design to mugs. (Left) Plain, 'VR', c.1890. (Right) A very heavy pint, with pronounced punt, not marked, possibly pre-1880.

Left and above: *It is rarely possible to recognise a particular glass in a picture as they are usually an incidental part of the scene and the artist was not concerned with accuracy of this item. This is a specific Victorian design shown on a brewery poster of 1911.*

Right and below: *A beaker of a popular design that lasted until the Second World War, shown in a brewery advertisement of 1895.*

Above and right: *The tulip and the Nonic pint, variations on the beaker. 'Nonic' is a strange trade name for the straight tapered glass with a slight bulge close to the rim, intended to aid the grip.*

Modern development of the beaker. Proprietary moulds. The Kronenbourg is embossed '1664' round the base, an excellent design feature in glass but rarely used.

Today's leading style, the beaker has ousted the mug. Ever taller and more spectacular designs use the possibilities of strong, thin modern glass.

Old Saxon origin. There have been some notable evolutions of style, as the illustrations show. The straight-sided mug went through a gradual evolution from Victorian times until the 1940s and then was suddenly displaced by the dimple, a mug with all-over thumb-print size indentations. These are common on earlier flutes and goblets but had not before appeared on a mug. The beaker was always present alongside the mug and today is the most successful design. Judging by the number of goblets surviving, this was the most popular style for a half pint throughout Victorian times. The plain style was known as a 'hob-nob', a description still found in catalogues today for tumblers. The name arises from the custom of 'hob and nobbing', alternately and repeatedly drinking one another's health, a term which we now use to denote mild sycophancy. The style has fallen out of favour today, being represented only by the special glasses for Belgian beers.

Verification today

All Britain's local authorities retain a weights and measures department and in the past those with manufacturers of mugs in their area were responsible for their verification. Staffordshire, with its heavy concentration of potteries, had a particularly large inspectorate. Today, however, there are no

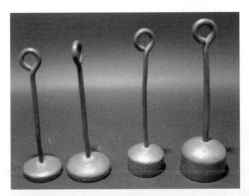

Verification in action. This machine, built around 1900, delivers exactly measured pints. It was once a requirement that every glass should be checked in this way. Today only a certain frequency of sampling is required as accuracy in modern glassmaking is more reliable. The plungers are 'allowances' of specific volume. A brim measure is allowed a tolerance in excess only, up to 34 ml. The plunger is inserted into any glass that still has headroom after filling with a pint. If it now overflows it is acceptable; if it does not it is rejected as too big. Pint-to-line glasses are allowed to be plus or minus half this amount either side of the line. The set of four plungers are 10 ml, 17 ml, 20 ml and 34 ml for checking half pints and pints.

Verification in action. (Left) Metal stencils used for sand-blasting. (Centre left) Modern rubber stencils. These accommodate to any diameter of glass whereas metal has to be custom-formed. (Centre right and bottom) A sand-blasting machine. The glass is bedded on to the stencil, the operator stamps her foot and releases a blast of compressed air and sand.

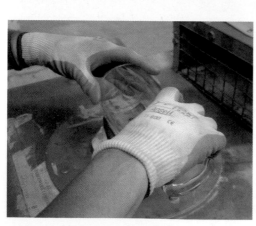

Above: *The perfect pint. It is not technically possible to obtain a perfectly measured pint using an ordinary jug or mug. The meniscus creates a saucer-shaped depression and the surface tension of water allows liquid to rise above the brim. The close-fitting lid with a hole in the centre is placed on top of the liquid, squeezing out any surplus into the central saucer, from where it can be removed.*

Right: *Verification punches used by inspectors for stamping pewter mugs.*

A mug showing repeated stamping from what appears to be an annual inspection. Pewter mugs were suspect as any dent reduced the capacity. It is marked 'GR6' – Glasgow Council doing a thorough job for its citizens.

Condemned! A rejected mug that has been stamped several times, with the word 'condemned' and trodden on. Someone has nevertheless reshaped it for further use.

longer any producers of pub beer mugs or glasses in the United Kingdom and only Bury Metropolitan Council retains its Glass Verification Centre. The main continental companies mark their glasses at manufacture under self-verification schemes approved by the National Weights and Measures Laboratory at Teddington. The Bury facility is maintained for smaller producers and smaller batches of special glasses.

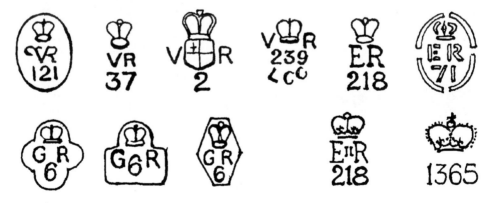

Some verification stamps incorporating the royal cipher, as used on beer mugs and other items at various times between 1879 and 1969. (From the Shire Album 'Weights and Measures' by J. T. Graham, third edition, 1993.)

The end of the mug
and the pint

The mug is in the process of becoming history. There was a time when barmen would ask if you wanted a handle or a straight glass (and this may still occasionally happen), but your beer will almost certainly be served today in a beaker. This change of fashion is being driven by innovative designs from larger continental brands, with a corresponding dearth of innovation from British breweries, few of which are big enough to commission their own moulds, the rest having to be content with badging the now old-fashioned nonic and tulip pints (see illustration on page 53).

With the demise of Ravenhead Glassworks of St Helens and Dema Glass of Chesterfield in 2001, pub glasses are no longer produced in England, but they are made on the Continent by Durabor in Belgium, Arcoroc in France and Pasabahce in Turkey. Their concerns are entirely dominated by European needs, not the local market of the United Kingdom, and the motive force behind new mug designs has now gone.

No government will wish to incur the stigma of abolishing the pint, but disuse is likely to come about by displacement. Were a test case to be brought against any British publican selling draught beer by the half litre, the law would almost certainly rule that United Kingdom law cannot take precedence over European Union law. Without abolishing the pint, this would open the way for metric measures, which would be welcomed by the large companies, which incur the extra cost of special arrangements for Britain. The pint would then hold out in a small number of real ale pubs, until the glassware ran out! It might eventually be a case of 'If you want a pint, bring your own mug'.

Collectors must do their own hunting for mugs as there are no specialist dealers offering a selection and they hardly ever appear in antique shops. They do, however, surface at the specialist glass fairs, the 'breweriana' auctions at Elsecar and on E-bay. Mochaware and pewter are in fairly plentiful supply and offer the best fields for an inexpensive collection. Victorian pint glasses are surprisingly rare, and early stoneware is generally a museum item.

Appendix 1: Summary of standard gallons

Ale gallon, 282 cubic inches. Probably derived from the ancient gallon by taking ten measures for eight.

Ancient gallon at the Guildhall, 224 cubic inches. This was based on 8 Tower pounds of wheat (as used by the Royal Mint at the Tower of London).

Corn gallon of Henry VII, 268 cubic inches.

Irish gallon, 224 or 217 cubic inches.

Scottish ale gallon, 311 cubic inches.

Scottish wine gallon, 467 cubic inches, equivalent to two English wine gallons.

Wine gallon, 233 cubic inches, derived from the French tun of wine. Given a statutory definition by Queen Anne as the volume of a cylindrical vessel 7 inches in diameter by 6 inches high (= 231 cubic inches).

Comparison chart for pints and customary measures

	Cubic inches	Fluid ounces	Millilitres
Ale gallon	282	163	4629
Ale pint		20.37	578
Wine gallon	231	133.5	3792
Wine pint		16.7	474
Imperial gallon	276.8	160	4544
Imperial quart		40	1136
Imperial pint		20	568
Imperial half-pint		10	284
Imperial gill		5	142
Imperial one third of a quart		13.3	378
Imperial one third of a pint		6.7	189
Imperial three quarters of a pint		15	426
Imperial 18 ounce pint		18	511
Scottish Stirling pint	103.8	55	1562
Scottish chopin		27.5	781
Scottish mutchkin		13.75	390
Irish gallon	217.6	125.8	3572
Irish pint		15.7	446

Appendix 2: Chronology of marking legislation and practice

1699. 11 and 12 William III c15. An Act for Ascertaining the Measures for Retailing Ale and Beer. Many stoneware mugs are found with the impressed mark WR and crown. With the death of William III some potters changed the royal cipher to AR and then GR. However, the law had not provided for a change of monarch and on strict interpretation WR was correct and remained so until this statute was repealed in 1867. The WR mark is not therefore reliable for dating to William III. Mochaware and glass mugs would in principle be similarly marked, but none has been found.

1824. 5 George IV c74. Weights and Measures Act. This introduced the imperial system and abolished the wine gallon and ale gallon. By implication this superseded the 1699 Act as the ale standard was no longer applicable. However, no specific instructions were issued about imperial marking and this is a time of much confusion.

1835. 5 and 6 William IV c63. Weights and Measures Act. This Act specifically exempted glass and earthenware jugs and drinking cups from marking. It gave the customer the right to have his drink measured in a stamped vessel if he wished. It probably did no more than recognise existing practice, given the practical difficulties of marking. From this time can be found mugs with sprigs, metal bands or ink stamps guaranteeing a pint or stating 'Imperial'. These were voluntarily applied by potters or publicans, because it is likely that, given the existence of certified pewter mugs, respectable pubs and manufacturers would want to advertise their adherence to the standard.

1878. 41 and 42 Victoria c49. Weights and Measures Act. This reintroduced marking for all measures and prompted the introduction of the system of unified verification numbers allocated to local authorities. This Act took good effect, as marking by means of sand-blasting had become a practical proposition and all mugs are now found officially verified to the extent that if an item is not marked we can assume it was not for use in a pub. From around this time can be found interesting examples of old mugs re-verified using pewter bands or buttons or tags.

1907. SR and O 689 Weights and Measures Regulations. These provided for a retaining rim of up to 10 per cent of the marked volume to prevent spillage, the origin of line measures.

1963. SI No 1891 Weights and Measures (prescribed stamp) regulations. This gave a standard design of crown and added the requirement of a date.

1968. SI No 1615 Weights and Measures (prescribed stamp) regulations. This confirmed the design of a crown plus number. For the first time since 1699 the monarch's cipher is omitted.

SUMMARY OF MARKING

1700–1869	GR, AR, WR and crown
1879–1901	VR, crown and number
1901–1910	ER, crown and number
1910–1952	GR, crown and number
1953–1963	EIIR, crown and number
1963–1969	EIIR, crown, number and date
1969 to present	crown and number

Further reading

Connor, R. D. *The Weights and Measures of England*. HMSO, 1999.

Connor, R. D. *Weights and Measures in Scotland*. Scottish Museums, 2003.

Department of Trade and Industry. *Measures of Draught Beer and Cider*. Consultation paper, 2001. Summarises the head on beer controversy.

Gaimster, D. *German Stoneware 1200–1900*. Trustees of the British Museum, 1997. Includes a chapter on Britain.

Graham, J. T. (revised by Maurice Stevenson). *Weights and Measures*. Shire, third edition 1993, reprinted 2003. Contains a useful list of verification numbers.

Green, Chris. *John Dwight's Fulham Pottery*. English Heritage, 2001. An account of the excavation.

Hatcher, J., and Barker, T. C. *A History of British Pewter*. Longman, 1974.

Mountford, Arnold. *Staffordshire Salt-Glazed Stoneware*. Barrie & Jenkins, 1997.

Ricketts, Carl. *Marks and Marking of Weights and Measures of the British Isles*. Available only from the author (ferristin@aol.com). Comprehensive listing of local authority marks.

Sussman, Lynne. *Mocha, Banded, Cat's Eye and Other Factory Made Slipware*. Council for North Eastern Historical Archaeology. Boston University, 1997. Shows the simple practical methods by which patterns were produced.

Victoria and Albert Museum. *Browne Muggs*. 1985. Catalogue of an exhibition of stoneware organised by the museum, including a good selection of pub mugs.

When is a mug a measure? Any verified beer mug is also a measure but these two ordinary mugs have been sold specifically as measures by the addition of the words 'pint up to the coloured line'. The difference would have been in the capacity variation permitted at manufacture. Mugs were produced with fairly generous latitude but measures more strictly. The promise of precision offered here is not fulfilled. The red line is so close to the top that in practical use the brim becomes the measure, thereby assuring the customer a fractionally generous pint.

Places to visit

There is unfortunately no representative selection of pub mugs to be seen. Several museums have some mugs included in ceramic collections and many town museums display the local standards. Stoneware is the best represented, mochaware sparsely and glass not at all. The Potteries Museum has probably the broadest selection. The Museum of London is strong on London stoneware, as also are the British Museum and the Victoria and Albert Museum, which includes German stoneware. Nottingham Castle Museum has local stoneware, and the Ashmolean Museum has some very early ware. The Science Museum has the most comprehensive collection of standards, and Winchester Museum the most ancient.

Ashmolean Museum, Beaumont Street, Oxford OX1 2PH. Telephone: 01865 278000. Website: www.ashmolean.org
The British Museum, Great Russell Street, London WC1B 3DG. Telephone: 020 7323 8000. Website: www.thebritishmuseum.ac.uk
Museum of London, 150 London Wall, London EC2Y 5HN. Telephone: 0870 444 3852. Website: www.museumoflondon.org.uk
Nottingham Castle Museum, off Maid Marian Way, Nottingham NG1 6EL. Telephone: 0115 915 3700. Website: www.nottinghsmcity.gov.uk
The Potteries Museum and Art Gallery, Bethesda Street, Hanley, Stoke-on-Trent, Staffordshire ST1 3DW. Telephone: 01782 232323. Website: www.stoke.gov.uk/museums
The Science Museum, Exhibition Road, South Kensington, London SW7 2DD. Telephone: 0870 870 4868. Website: www.sciencemuseum.org.uk
Victoria and Albert Museum, Cromwell Road, South Kensington, London SW7 2RL. Telephone: 020 7942 2000. Website: www.vam.ac.uk
Westgate Museum, High Street, Winchester, Hampshire SO23 8ZB. Telephone: 01962 848269. Website: www.winchester.gov.uk

Badging. This is the method of personalising a standard glass by use of etching or paint transfer. It was economical enough to be used by larger pubs, breweries, railways and shipping lines. These two examples are about one hundred years apart: (left) Duffy & Co, The Palace, Ann Street, Belfast, c.1890; (right) Brakspear, Henley-on-Thames, c.1995.

Index